X
LA
Poets

Library of Congress Cataloging-in-Publication Data
Linda Ravenswood
X LA Poets
ISBN-978-1-7324848-3-2
Library of Congress Control Number: 2021907982

Copyrights

Editor: Linda Ravenswood
Foreword: Yago S. Cura
Cover Art: Autumn Anglin
Book Design: Autumn Anglin, www.greygirlgraphics.com
Illustrations: Autumn Anglin

©2021 HINCHAS Press
Los Angeles, California 90066
www.HINCHASpress.com

Printed and Bound by: IngramSpark

Printed in the United States of America

ISBN-978-1-7324848-3-2

X
LA
Poets

Edited by Linda Ravenswood

Foreword by Yago S. Cura

HINCHAS
Press

Los Angeles, California

ACKNOWLEDGMENTS

Arminé Iknadossian, "Resident Alien: A Memoir in Verse" first appeared in *Alabama Literary Review* in a different version, Volume 22, 2013

Rachel Kann, "Roses and Thunder" first appeared in *Hevria*, September 2019

Rachel Kann, "The Most Unkindest Cut of All" first appeared in *Hevria*, October 2017

Rachel Kann, "Jellyfish Dance of the Ten Infinities" first appeared in *Hevria*, March 2019

Rachel Kann, "Kindness / The Murmuration of Starlings" first appeared in *Hevria*, April 2018

Rachel Kann, "I Surrender" first appeared in *Hevria*, January 2019

Teresa Mei Chuc (Chúc Mỹ Tuệ), "Quan Âm on a Dragon" first appeared in *Whitefish Review*, Summer 2015

Teresa Mei Chuc (Chúc Mỹ Tuệ), "Cockroaches" was first appeared in the chapbook, *Cartesian Product* (Silkworms Ink)

Teresa Mei Chuc (Chúc Mỹ Tuệ), "Agent Blue" first appeared in *Kyoto Journal*, Summer 2015

Teresa Mei Chuc (Chúc Mỹ Tuệ), "I Took Nothing" first appeared in Rattle, Issue #44

Teresa Mei Chuc (Chúc Mỹ Tuệ), "Photosynthesis" first appeared in *EarthSpeak Magazine*

Viva Padilla, "xolo. a mi amante que ya no puede vivir debajo del capitalismo y la farsa de la democracia de los estados unidos" first appeared in *The Acentos Review*, Feb. 2020

Viva Padilla, "la extranjera" first appeared in *The Acentos Review*, Feb. 2020

Viva Padilla, "the destroyer woman" first appeared in *Brooklyn & Boyle*, Dec. 2017

Viva Padilla, "sueño americano, ni que nada" first appeared in *Cultural Weekly*, June 2020

Viva Padilla, "utilizing google maps to triangulate the course of my desmadre over the years" first appeared in *PANK Magazine*, July 2020

Linda Ravenswood, "Poetry is a Shapeshifter" first appeared in *Angels + Flight Literary West*, 2017, aflwmag.com/2017/01/23/poetry-shapeshifter/

Linda Ravenswood, "Gen X Suite" first appeared by *A-B Projects*, 2019

Linda Ravenswood, "If I was smart as an onion skin" first appeared in *The Hamilton Stone Review*, 2010, www.hamiltonstone.org/hsr21.html

CONTENTS

Shonda Buchanan

Teresa Mei Chuc (Chúc Mỹ Tuệ)

Viva Padilla

Chelsea Rector

Linda Ravenswood

from Linda: for my mother y papa. for my children. and for Stanley.

from Yago: to Panda, Berlin, and Cy for giving me the confidence to orchestrate.

FOREWORD

by Yago S. Cura

Linda, Arminé and I are members of Project 1521, a group of artists and writers started by painter, Sandy Rodriguez, and Taco Shop Poet and radio journalist, Adolfo Guzman-Lopez. Our workshop attempts to make sense of the future by studying the texts of the past.

In particular, our workshop discusses the production, aesthetic, and techniques and concepts found inside Bernardino de Sahagúns 12 volume, 2,400 page compilation, *Historia general de las cosas de la Nueva España*. Also known as the Florentine Codex, the text serves as a textual talisman for the members of our group as it literally records the destruction of the Aztec/Mexica empire. Likewise, Linda and I geeked out over typewriters, and the legacy of Miriam Matthews, the first credentialed African-American librarian hired by the Los Angeles Public Library. We found ourselves in awe, and at her altar, because Miriam plied her trade for the LAPL at a time when she was the only person of color in every room all of the time!

Linda and I built an index of libraries that hire performers and built a super femmed out volume so that women of color were emphasized. We thought a print edition would be keen since we were going for maximum usability. We had several outstanding mice-plans, all of which were body-slammed by the pandemic.

I spoke with Linda and we decided to put the project with the namesake on hold, or at least switch it over to the digital world, and proceed with another project: *X LA Poets*.

X LA Poets is purposeful pachanga, a poetry anthology synchronized by all carriers and blessed by Los Angeles agents. As such, we intended this book to brim with allusions, namesakes, and tributes. Yes, we wanted to give a nod to punk band, X, whose album *Los Angeles* (1980) is indelibly etched into the genetic code of this collection. But, the intersecting search lights on the cover also allude to the idea of Los Angeles as a landscape of widespread spectacle, full of danger and artifice (and production value.) Even greater sources of inspiration turned out to be *8 Miami Poets* (Jai Alai Books, 2016) the music of Polly Jean Harvey (especially the 1993 album, *Rid of Me*) and Miriam Matthews, the inexorable backbone of this endeavor, guiding us from the never-before-seen to the beyond-beyond.

INTRODUCTION

Linda Ravenswood

From the unceded lands of The Tongva, Gabrielino, Hahamongna, Tataviam, Kavwevitam.

1521-2021 — The Quincentenary of The Spanish Conquest of Tenōchtitlan

03-19-2021

Thanks so much for picking up this book. As I compose the introduction, we're still in global-pandemic-lockdown due to Covid 19. Today is the one-year anniversary of that strange new oblivion for us in Los Angeles. In times like these, the generations explore art, words, dances, and songs — to remember — to spell and pray to be delivered to better days. We hope for what Asghar, Keats, Shelley, Anzaldua, Virgil, Kinnell, Heaney, Borges, Barthes, Sze, Smith, Shangé, Plath & Hughes, Phranc & Lisa, Hall & Kenyon, Ginsberg & Orlovsky, Cage & Cunningham, Luis y Trini, Miller & Morath, Jean-Paul et Simone hope for — the chance to work. *To make.*

I'd like to say thanks to several people who made room for books and made room for kids in L.A. like me, who wanted to be with books: **Leigh Peffer** from Wilshire Books in Santa Monica. In the dark aisles he curated I found my people, my métier. **Doug Dutton** who ran Dutton's in Brentwood, and employed my teacher & friend **Scott Wannberg**. Scott helped me find books, and writers. Scott ushered me into the LA Poetry world & I read in coffee houses with him from the time

I was a teen-ager. **Rabbi Alfred Wolf and Rebbetzin Wolf** of Congregation B'nai B'rith, at The Wilshire Boulevard Temple, **and their sons**, who entrusted me with their parent's library in 2004. My grandmother **Dorothy Lois Everson McKee** and her third husband (who I called Grandpa) **Larkin Wray**, the well respected Los Angeles book dealer. My grandmother, an Oregon native, owned movie theatres with my grandfather **Hugh McKee** through the mid 20th century. Best known among their acquisitions are The Clinton Theatre & Hotel in Portland, and The Montrose Theatre in Los Angeles. Later, she and her third husband helmed Antiques Et Cetera on Fountain in Los Feliz. They must've brought home 30,000 books and ephemera for me. **Philip Alan Evans & Bjorg Knudsen (Bibbi Evans)**, my Aunt Bibbi and Uncle Phil, book lovers and first friends, who told me my voice was important, and valuable. **Jim Duda & Jonathan Rios**, who supported me in publishing, and continue to fund The Los Angeles Press. To all the institutions and civic partners across the country who have hired me, allowing me to live in my native city and support my children — especially: The 24th Street Theatre, Angels Gate Cultural Arts Centre, The WCCW, The Poetry Society of New York, Red Light Lit, Asylum Arts and American Jewish University, LACE, PEN America, The City of West Hollywood, RentPoet Brian Sonia-Wallace & Melrose Poetry Bureau, and The LAPL. To the hundreds of **writers & artists** I've worked with in Los Angeles, NYC, & San Francisco — thank you for continuing the artist's pilgrimage with me.

The artists assembled in this book are all authentically L.A. —

Teresa Mei Chuc (Chúc Mỹ Tuệ)'s family relocated

to California from Saigon, VietNam in the 1970's. I first encountered her stunning artwork in my local bookshop, Skylight Books in Los Feliz, around 2002. Her homage to her grandma, *Gladiola*, was a chapbook, then a short film. It is a stunning and glorious piece of art. I kept trying to locate her, and finally in 2008, found her email and wrote to tell her how much I appreciated her ethos. She sent me all of her books and chapbooks *gratis*, in solidarity and friendship. Teresa's poems depict voyages on mighty ships, not knowing if or where they'll land. Her poetry is infused with memory; the work of human hands on fibers, plants, bowls, soil; and the beauty and ancient knowledge of people on multiple continents. Her paternal grandmother planted seeds of orange trees in Los Angeles that still bear fruit every year. Teresa shares those fruits generously, as she shares her rich, loam-like poems. Dark poems. Light poems. Necessary poems. Not surprisingly, Teresa was named Poet Laureate of her town, Altadena, California in 2018. She continues her family legacies of service as an editor, land steward, gardener, community activist, martial artist, caretaker, cook, teacher, poet, friend.

Chelsea Rector is an L.A. native daughter, cowgirl, dog walker, KTown performance artist, philosopher, singer and voice artist. Chelsea makes new words and worlds in literature. A combination of philosophy, recipe, and song, her poems are mini-histories and stand alone lexicons. She presents like a young Elizabeth Taylor, but then you look down and she's wearing water skis under her dress. She's more than glad to tell you why, based on a quote from Derrida. Her writing and live performance are funny, and profound. She takes herself lightly, humbly; but her work is powerful, and what she's attempting is serious business. Chelsea contends with the voluminosity of language and thought, and her work wrestles within aeons of art and literature — drawing from The Greeks, French Literary Theory, Music and Essay. The first broadside The Los Angeles Press made in 2018 was a discourse of Chelsea's on Poetics.

Viva Padilla started the literary journal *Dryland* in 2015 to bring focus to artists and writers from her hometown, South Central L.A. In *XLA* she shares poetry in Spanish and English. Visions — 'outsiders' locating themselves on streets, neighbourhoods, and vast expanses of desert; border-crossers of both geography and spirit — gather in her poems. She finds herself reflected in her father's journey and struggle, and that mirror is a blessing, but also a song of heartbreak. I was very honoured to translate some of her work from Spanish to English. Her work stands in lineage with Cherríe Moraga, Gloria Anzaldua, and Gloria Enedina Alvarez.

I met **Arminé Iknadossian** when she was running the bookstore at Beyond Baroque in Venice. Her poetry will bring you a gift-image of mulberries and wine. Her poems, like others in this collection, tell of transcontinental voyages, and children fleeing government-made catastrophes. Her histories of migration and the ensuing years of sifting those trajectories perform a healing ceremony of global connectivity.

Rachel Kann is a poet, dancer and Kohenet. I met her on a green escarpment above L.A. in 2017. We were making a short film for Make Music L.A. and she stood with musicians and poets, calling home blessings in the green wind. Rachel's poems are prayers and dances invoking the mystery and the mystic. Sometimes her poems read like songs, and they move in lineage with Rumi, Mirabai, Emily Dickinson, Wiliam Blake, Walt Whitman, and Hannah Rachel Verbermacher.

As we were going to press with *XLA*, **Lynne Thompson** was named Poet Laureate of Los Angeles. After decades of work and service, it's fantastic that Lynne's voice and dedication to letters is being lifted so high. As the first poet among us civically, we'll continue to look to Lynne to guide and shape the ways poetry can hold and share our histories and dreams. The poems she blesses us with in *XLA* keep the names and histories of our country, from the South to the Southland, most profoundly in Sandra Bland, and Breonna Taylor. Lynnes's poetry connects us to the global histories of art and music as well, reaching to Greek Mythology, and to masters of her genre, James Baldwin, and James Joyce. To me, Lynne's poems read like micro-monographs, or sublime journal entries from a tender, unseen friend, closely watching us as we make our way around the city.

When you read **Allison Hedge Coke's** poetry in *XLA*, you're offered an account of The City of Angels from the 1950's to the present. Allison's poems of LA relate trips around town with celebrities, forgotten cemeteries, and being spun in a city of cars. Her witness tells of the headiness of LA in the 90's, and the whimsicality of our city in the 1950's. Her work shares a sense of possibility and return to — if not innocence, then a hope to experience mobility, vigour, and sunshine again. Allison's Hollywood poetry intersects traditional LA climes with an even more ancient reality, the people on whose lands all the glitz was built. Her poetry includes the often unheard parallel histories of N8iV and NDN artists, actors, writers, and sportspeople in our city.

Luivette Resto's poetry in *XLA* is part kitchen ballad and part aubade & always on a current that rides socio-political and revolutionary points of view. In her poems, she details learning to speak English by watching soap operas, and how she strut school corridors with that new language as a shield and weapon. Her poems are fiery claims. For all of her witness, her poems are not acts of reception, but of defiance. Her poems outline new maps, in love and life. Her poems delineate where she will go, and where others must take care not to trespass. Her poems remind us to stake a claim, stand up, and hold on to authentic self.

Among the many books **Shonda Buchanan** has published, it's her 2017 anthology *Voices from Leimert Park Redux* that exemplifies an LA poetry manual. In it, she requests artists to reflect on an LA below The Ballona Wetlands, below the 10 fwy, a part of town ringed by a confluence of Black and Brown histories. Shonda's publishing career highlights the many times she's lifted up community stories. Her writing mirrors this sacred placemaking. In her poems, you feel as if you're on a slow drive with her around LA, as she drops boys names, girls names, memories, missed connections, grandmothers, grocery stores, piano music, fallen friends back into the landscape where they always should have been but were removed, often violently, shamefully. As a writer of mixed ancestry, her poetry walks within multi-foliate worlds, offering reflections on essential Native American and Black Indian perspectives. Shonda's stewardship in publishing urges us to Say Her Name. Her legacy is a fierce prayer of protection, and hope.

The writers in *XLA* are allied on many fronts: we're women and womyn identifying writers, and all of us call Los Angeles home. Some of our ancestors have been in LA through centuries, some of us are immigrants, asylum seekers, and first generation Americans. We are Beirutsees, Chicanas y Xicanxs, Irish, Mexicanas, Jews, Boriquas, Vietnamese, Native Americans, Black NDN's, Europeans, and the grandchildren of slaves. We're also poets laureate, artists, professors, reporters, mothers, publishers, business owners, warriors, feminists, and partners towards the Emergent Ecocene.

What all of us have in common is *the book*. One could argue it's not our gender, our Latinidad, our refugee status, our Q/BIPOC affiliations, or even the city itself that compels us here. But — *the book*. And not just this book, perhaps not even our shared genre — poetry that summons us. We live, and work specifically with books because our generations lived and worked *con historias y cuentos*, and made sharing that awe and reverence for story a part of the tradition of our family. We are a community of writers — a community of the book. Yago and I thank you for reading, teaching, and sharing the poetry of *XLA*.

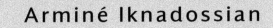

Arminé Iknadossian

Resident Alien: A Memoir in Verse

1.
The Becca Valley was a patchwork
of orange and olive trees.

Time and again
war saw its own becoming.
Time and again
a girl was born.

During the first trimester
before the sex has mutated
into its primal evocation
Mother craved sweets and bitters alike.

Like shafts of moonlight.
Like tangled bed sheets.
Like ripped stockings and fault lines.

2.
Mother's water broke
before Watergate.
It became apparent
Beirut would have the same fate.

Like trying to run underwater
childhood was awkward and slow.
But war makes sure to make men
out of little girls.

3.

The morning after curfew
I sit between my parents
while we drive through West Beirut.

We need cash for diapers,
formula, groceries.

Joy follows death to the back room.
They make a baby
and call it Beirut.

Even in this city
of incredulity, Derrida
lives in the asphalt without irony.

Men who fear mold more than RPGs.
That kind of pathology.

Sons and daughters
of Khalil. We are called *Beirutsees*

because we live like we die,
with eyes wide open.

Not like drunken poets.
But civilized like
intentional brushfires.

Lament

- for Black Lives Matter

Dead songs lie on the floor like flat palm leaves.
I hold their green hands and weep from my mouth.

I was born from women ground into flour,
in a country with so much solemn wheat.

Our loaves are heavy with disaster.
We make books from bread,

dip a hand in holy water to sprinkle
the last page, keep it wet with worry.

Without our songs, who would we be?
What will our last page say with its alphabet of blackened
teeth?

We serve our songs under aspic and sliced lemon
so you know what you are about to eat.

Maybe the right song will lift the white sheet off our wailing.
Here is a song for arthritic hands,

all those years the moon's face a white sheet.
I stand silent in the heat, turning dark like a piece of fruit.

Who will hurl their songs to the sky flat as a failed promise?
What will we do now, with so many *friends* you cannot count
the daggers?

For Olives

In Greek mythology, olives were a gift to humankind by the goddess Athena.

They rained from the trees in Santa Ana Winds.
My mother, every weekend, bed sheets ready in the trunk of her car,
drove to my high school, laid the sheets under the trees,
shook them, or simply gathered the fallen,

tossed them by the handful into plastic bags.
Large jars of water, salt, vinegar, lemon, thyme, and garlic.
Mother craved olives every day of her pregnancy.
I was born with an olive-shaped birthmark on my calf.

Leave them brining a week or two, the longer the sweeter.
Warm pita over a burner. Slice tomato,
fresh mint from the side garden. Dirt under nails.
Pits into palms, spoons, napkins. Wrinkled-black Greek ones,

Turkish green, Kalamata, Mission. A clutch of green onions
next to the mint, a small dish for the pits. A pit in the stomach
grows a tree. A tree is a home. Rain fed, dirt fed, sun fed.
A woman feeds her family with what she gathers in her arms.

My family ate them after every meal, crushed them into paste,
made whole meals out of them when meat was scarce. Olives keep well.
In the trunk of my mother's car, you will always find:
a jar of olives, a change of clothes, and running shoes.

The New Migration

Where this time, my daughter?
(We) lost two cities, lovely ones,
Elizabeth Bishop wrote.

Some of us are "lucky" in
that we have family
in the wide diaspora

of homelessness.
So coming November,
when the elections turn violent,

we know what to do.
We are packing,
shedding nonessentials,

notifying family in
Canada, Amsterdam, Argentina.
Here we are

in the united
suffering of America,
where, Saul Williams wrote, *the greatest*
Americans have not been born
yet.

Croatia? I ask my mother.
Your best friend is there.
Maybe she will let us live on her land
til we get on our feet.

Too close to Russia, she replies.
We made that mistake before.

Rachel Kann

Roses and Thunder

יש and roses and thunder.
את and jasmine and metamorphosis.

Who is this Eve?
What garden does she haunt?
Where is the lethal serpent
everyone speaks of?
What snap of bite into apple
cracks through ruby skin,
firm to bursting?

What crisp white flesh is this?
What sweetness
drips down her chin?

What is this churning of earth
beneath her dusty feet?

What florid, black richness
creeps between her toes,
beckons her shins,
calves, knees, hips?

Who placed these angels—
meant to terrify—
upon the lintel,
swords aflame and spinning?

Whose hand opens the gate
and locks it fast again?

Who pierces this dome of night?

What bloodsister infinity-of-pinpricks
on her indigo palm
releases lily streamers to unfurl
and dangle with
the lusciousness of temptation?

The Most Unkindest Cut of All

...For Brutus, as you know, was Caesar's angel:
Judge, O you gods, how dearly Caesar loved him!
This was the most unkindest cut of all;
For when the noble Caesar saw him stab,
Ingratitude, more strong than traitors' arms,
Quite vanquish'd him: then burst his mighty heart...
—Shakespeare, Julius Caesar

You are a violent glamour,
a dagger
carved from obsidian.

Your style of warpaint
never changes, but
neither does the truth:

I am the one
you have let see you,
barefaced,
clean,
naked,
unshielded
and soft
blotched
as a newborn's cheek.

You are still a cruel thing,
having only grown in meanness
in the interim,

judgmental as a fundamentalist,

unpredictable as wind,
beautiful as moonlight.

You are a one-woman coven
on a witchhunt,
a preemptive code-switch,
a walking, talking
shoot-first-or-get-shot.

How does it feel
to lay your head
upon your pillow
each night
and know

that those
who love you
do so
out of fear
of your capricious
and tempestuous wrath;

to know your every relationship
is built on a flimsy foundation
of shallow respect
earned through intimidation?

You are a schoolyard bully
costumed as a grown up.

Let your devotees continue
to lay rubies and switchblades
at your feet—

lipstick and black incense
upon your tear and bloodstained altar—

I have no taste for recruitment.

I keep my distance by design.

I know
what lies within
the coiled spring of shield
you hide inside,

the sweet and whimpering
child who can't believe
she's good,

deserving of
fearless love.

Jellyfish Dance of the Ten Infinities

Shekhinah is gathering
all the female fallen sparks
to her sacred darkness,

a cosmological, spiraling,
majesty of literal crystal dust
that opalescents
in jellyfish heartbeat bellows;

I am grateful
to this seeming-stillness,
which allows these
ten infinities
their full and
paradoxical expansion.

Find me
lost in orchards,
sweet-talking
peach blossoms.

Each trial by fiery furnace,
each truth by blue ocean—

sing praise to
the tried-and-true soul.

Kindness / The Murmuration of Starlings

Be kind, for everyone you meet is fighting a hard battle.
—Philo of Alexandria

Have your heard of murmuration?
Listen, it's breathtaking.

It's basically bird-flocking quantified
to the awesomest power.

It's starlings—
communing through flying and swirling—
like one transcendent entity.

They move in a fluid choreographic flux
on the constant edge of *next shift,*
next shift, next shift,

and each of these shifts
is called a *critical transition,*

a murmuration of thousands of starlings,
tuned to each other's movement through
phenomena of scale-free correlation,
following neighboring velocities,

each bird affecting
the next seven birds nearest them,
and the next seven, and the next seven.
Look, even Charles Darwin said *survival of the fittest*

was a misapprehension of his findings,
even he believed in the holistic,
was awed by the elaborate and elegant
interdependence of nature.

From abiogenesis all the way to present-day,
from subatomic particles to the entire biosphere,
it's emergence that encourages evolution.

Kill or be killed is a lie of the mind.
An outdated paradigm.
A flak jacket that can't keep out light.

Let us take flight
toward our final destination
of wild and untamable
kindness.

The voyage is long
and travels forward
and backward in time.
It's a bumpy ride,
but the upshot is, we can't not try.

I'm talking directly to
the little you
who lives inside you,

reminding you of all the truth
you once *knew* you knew implicitly,
returning you to your previous innocence,
restoring your clarity,
because kindness is your true nature,

and I promise, anything beyond that
has been inculcated.

Truthfully,
separation itself is an illusion
double-brewed
in a hateful culture-stew
of roiling cruelty
we've all been cooking in.

And despite the desire to stay in denial,
it's bubbling to the surface.

What I'm saying is,
there's way more work for us to do.
Don't get lulled into complacency
by that fact that you *feel* compassion.

Kindness is action.
Not just that, as a matter of fact,
kindness is actually a radical act
in this hardscrabble and roughshod
crapshoot sneak-attack of a life
spilling with inner demons
and double-dealings.

Kindness transcends mere feelings,
it digs in the dirt,
is braver than hurled insults,
is rebellious enough to be vulnerable,
is vulnerable enough to rebel,
is confident enough to be patient,
calls forth a great recalibration,

an attunement to the taste
of sweetness
that starts within.

If you're currently
in life's trenches,
please get this:

kindness is
your weapon,
your best defense,
your greatest defiance.
This ain't rocket science.
I don't care what your tribe is.
The surprise is that
kindness does not equal weakness.

Actually, it's meanness
that requires an Achilles' heel to sting.

Do not be deceived,
meanness preys on insecurity,
offers false surety,
walls off and masks,
distracts from the voice inside
calling for acknowledgement,
needful of healing.

All neglect and emotional starvation is
based on pattern repetition so ancient,
it's trodden
raw and bloody
crop circles

upon your throbbing heart.

Behind every protective wall of defensiveness
is a frightened child fearing for their very life.

Do not withhold the kindness
that is longing to flow through you.

Give it away. Now.

Be courageous enough to topple facades,
repurpose them to bridges,
span divisions.

Once you've been on the brink,
stared in the abyss, no matter the flavor
of your personal chasm of darkness,
kindness becomes your soul's own prerequisite.
Once you've been to the bottom,
you can recognize salvation
in simplicity:

the merciful intoxication
from the swoon-perfume
of orange blossoms.

The awe possible from
a sky ablaze with the
murmuration of starlings.

The heartrending generosity
of unguarded eye contact.

This injurious journey
is filled with hair-triggered-
human-ticking-trauma-bombs,
who only want love
in a way they can understand it,

waiting for someone to say
show me where it hurts
and give them
the chance
to answer.

Do not withhold the kindness
that is longing to flow through you.

In this very moment,
choose to say *yes*,
remember gentleness,
even toward you,
though you like it rough,
even though life's made you tough,
choose to stop all the naysaying.
Who are you to discourage anyone,
yourself very much included?
Choose to be grace.
Choose the alchemy
that awaits your bravery,
spin your entire existence
into endless golden thread.

In this very moment,
choose to say *yes*,
put your hand on your chest—

on your heart,
on your throat,
on your cheek,

let that voice
within you speak,

and this time, listen,
give yourself the gift of presence,

in this very moment,
choose to say yes,
let this newfound gift
of presence warm like caramel
taffy in your hands,
let it expand wider

to encompass the person
in front of you,
behind you,
to each side of you,

the seven people closest to you,
the next seven,
and the next seven, and the next,
past the four walls of any room and
let it grow in your inclusion,
past human,
past all blooming,
past every last murmuration of starlings,
until your soul is a swarm of moonbeams,
filling the universe
with your unique,

super-sweet
and deeply-needed
illumination.

I Surrender

to the mystery,
to the undertow,
the sonic boom,
the solitude,
the blindness that might
or might not precede second sight,

every moonbeamy dream,
every starry-eyed vision,
every last second
spent in sweet anticipation,
every restless breath,
every expectation,

my dignity,
my faith,
my long-expired fire,
quirk and desire,
my want of belonging,
my longing to understand,

to the stamina
this resistance
presses against me with,
to the gravity of gravity
and the graveness of graves,

to the solitude,
to the sonic boom,
the undertow,
the mystery,

I surrender.

Lynne Thompson

Delusion, An Urban Romance

We live in a city ringed with false teeth.
We don't know we are living.

We're dreaming, forgetting
dreams have meaning conjoined

to tinsel and modern catastrophes.
We exhale by a sea

the color of guilt and broken jade,
the life of its whales

a slaughter of notes we cannot name.
We can't begin again anywhere else

and since the only tradition is to err,
we live on memory & Bibb lettuce and

when life falls from sequence to drift-
wood, we linger, we legends of ruin.

Dirge for Murdered Black Girls

for Sandra Bland and Breonna Taylor

How lovely the ruins.
Our beloveds. You, ever you—
(how ruined the lovely)—are

America's most unbearable fear subject to
stealth, to a Judas kiss turned ambush.
How lovely the ruins

we can't pretend we don't see: our could-have-been-
anything-they-wanted snuffed out like wicks.
How ruined the lovely.

How anguished the left behind:
the mothers, mourners, the others just like them.
How lovely the ruins,

the promise gone from should have been,
the girls laughing, dreaming of, calling out "see you later".
How ruined our once-lovely thoughts.

We know this anguish continues to happen
from Chattahoochee to the City of Angels.
How ruined the lovely—
who some think unlovely—how?

The Blue Haze

thinking of Terrance Hayes

They're like those moonstruck
  gypsy-gals who gave Apollo a one-
    eye; who coaxed canonical intrigue.

They are a slippery crew—
  blue in their gyre,
    blue-black like maggots

and never sexless. They invent
  a contagion when they steam,
    when they revenge.

Jesus, what an irony!—
  these women most holy
    when wet, these sister-girls

who splash suspicion over a meadow—
  phoebe babies lost to their mothers,
    quislings with no country,

They won't mark time in a vestibule.
  They can't wait to un-tame jive.
    They violet. They violet and violet.

Purgatorio

Once there was a girl who ate paper but not just any paper—
no Macy's receipts or mattress tags, she preferred Proust for
breakfast, a little Tolstoy on toast. During school recesses, she
was seen gnawing on The Weary Blues. Always bored by just
one thing, she devoted the seasons to variety: Shakespeare
in spring, of course, and always, Pushkin in December, every
other year. Every other year, she left luck to chance. In `92,
the holidays were all James'—Henry, Joyce, and Baldwin. The
family was a little put out. Harrumphs and tongues clacking
were heard across the dinner table. In photos, her image
looked like The Color Purple's Celie. All she knew was that
everything on earth was a-bristle. One year, she disappeared
altogether. There's even a tale, (tall-in-the-telling we're sure)
that when she finally took a merchant for a lover, she hid
Sonnets to Orpheus beneath his pillow which he tolerated
until he found Death of a Salesman atop the tank of the
john and fled. Recently, she was spotted in serene repose on
a California beach, a tattered copy of The Myth of Sisyphus
clutched between her teeth.

Veal

When your lover slides on top of you, smooth as a buzz saw,
that's when your throat contracts with the yellow dog ditty
you recognize as here comes trouble. This is not about playing

the dozens. This is fact. And you can catalog sixteen reasons
for suspicion. You karaoke Ray Charles crying Born to Lose;
bongo the distinct death-knell of some primitive's dry heave.

This is the time to waylay your lover's monosyllabics; to see
he's only the burnt residue of a cock-a-doodle-duh! And trust
this: even the cocks will sympathize knowing all the days after

will leave you with nothing but pinot get-real and poetry work-
shops. This is life, geechee girl—being picked over like black market
veal. The cosmos is determined to deep-fry you until you turn up leather.

You won't rise like a phoenix because day never follows a cataclysm
and you're just like Lena Horne without a room in Alabama, 1935.
So pass on the blind man's bluff. Start crooning the Stale Meat Blues.

Allison Hedge Coke

Downtown '58

Like Angels Flight clung to Bunker Hill incline
Exiles hung to night's belly until dawn dislodged
Opened wide sky over peak of patter horn.
They rose with crow's eyes, under Santa Anas.
Fought with teeth bared, broken nosed relocation
                                    upper cut thrown.

La Brea & Melrose

Nothing's perfect, never was,
except that time Brenda Swanson
was dating Julian Lennon, modeling
L'eggs or *No Nonsense*, driving
Robert Wagner's convertible
from her bestie Katie, took us
to lunch with Julian who picked
up all our tabs, in the car, hood
down, when we believed in anything.

Oakwood, Departed

for Dehl

At the end, we wondered if some of the Tongva,
buried next door, in traditional cemetery
long unmarked by fire, were laughing
chuckling sight of this.   If you, too,   laughing.

Though one stayed home contemplating
                her love made death of you.
The fountain near the prep sprayed two
of your exes in their faces. Three attended.

All stood and wailed a bit, maybe the only
time they were somewhere in unison,
like swans somehow along the graveside.

Made us laugh a bit at the absurdity, as
scattering cars scurried into lean lines.
Cars from Rolls to lucky starts all appeared.
Rest assured we were moving a pace more
Old Santa Susana Stage Road nearby than
freeway.

Out of them tumbled such a disparate
bunch, one might wonder who could bring
them all together, unless they knew.

We felt your face hardened. Rock - like you
were for us in life. Hard — like you were
to anyone who might hurt us.

Threw our handfuls, sang,   departed.

Coliseum

Raiders games we paid gang kids
to keep eyes on, hands off our wheels.
Just blocks from Memorial Coliseum where we
could not afford to park, for crazy games
people called *Plunket! Plunket!* When Raiders
fans rallied the veteran player to take the field
again, and otherwise

we watched the fans sometimes more than
the game, as fights broke out over any slight,
carrying afternoon heat into sultry kick back.
Catching nuts, dogs, nachos, your little satin
sleeved Raiders jackets, from some clearance
or yard sale, shined in tungsten fashion, your
faces wide with smiles, surprise —

still with me. Like knowing Plunket's parents,
like your grandma, blind. Knowing he had blood
from somewhere south, was just enough to soar
every inch he made below the stands, every
centimeter.

Car was always washed por nada when we rounded
back to catch her. We'd tip what concessions left us,
take leave, hope we'd save enough to do it all again.

The Names

Our scene partners were Ernie Fragua,
Grant Brittan, Angelo Michael Masino,
on occasion we repped Kim Norris,
Zahn McClarnon, Shirley Cheechoo,
Gary Farmer, Rodney Grant, Saginaw,
Jim Elk, Wes Studi, so many more.

Geiogomah's dance theater rocketed
still nights into constellated heavens.

Michael Horse curated artifacts, princess
telephones for the little white man museum
of Americana curiosities,   paving ways
for better suns.

Seems so long ago, a lifetime,
Will Sampson, Jesse Ed, Dehl, Trudell.

Luivette Resto

An Incomplete Ode to Older Brothers

To his sisters
if older brothers were poems

he'd be an ode
because sometimes older brothers

stand-in for absent fathers
at sweet sixteen dances

personify prince charming
on Valentine's Day with flowers & candies

symbolize strength when delivering tough conversations
that start: "Dad isn't coming for us"

giver of impromptu hugs, I love you's,
dinner & a movie dates

deliverer of patience and corny jokes
during driving lessons

odes are not for me
he'd argue, I am not special

but to them
he would always be

No More Poems

I will no longer write poems for you
I will only write them for me
odes calling me baby girl
ballads dancing with me in the kitchen
as I check on the beans simmering on the stove
sonnets filled with metaphors
about the heartiness of my unfeminine laugh
haikus holding my hand through Prospect Park in the fall
villanelles moaning my name as the refrain
and elegies for the unfinished verses

My Love Is a Continent

My love is a continent
an unconquerable land
absent of manifest destiny
no man's footprints, fingerprints
no flags planted on this body.

My love is a continent
pray on me
leave me *ofrendas*
de chicharrón y empanadas.

My love is a continent
cartographers have yet etched into history books.

My love is a continent
compartmentalized by states
named after my whims, dalliances, & lovers,
borderlines created by manicured fingertips.

My love is a continent
unnamed by the best etymologists.

My love is a continent
a sanctuary for women
un puerto para las malcriadas,
chingonas, cabronas, jefas,
y sin vergüenzas.

My love is a continent
for all of the outliers

and anomalies of this world,
the forgotten ones who live in the gray.

My love is a continent
without longitude and latitude lines
or vector points
you will not find my love on a map, GPS,
or Thomas Guide.

My love is a continent
legendary like the Pyramids
enigmatic like the Bermuda Triangle
unexplainable like your need to visit it over and over again.

My love is a continent
uncolonized by anyone's demands,
romances, or persuasions.

My love is a continent
I never want to give away.
I want to hold it in my arms
And shield it from the brutality of the sun.
May my love live uninhabited, uninhibited
For it can't ever be damaged
bruised, burned to the ground.

How Days of Our Lives Taught Me English

In 1982 Bo was in love with Hope
but she was promised to Larry Welch
a skeevy, lecherous politician.

In 1982 my abuela and I landed at JFK
greeted by tía, abuelo, and his maroon station wagon Impala
with its 8-track tapes and backwards third row.

In 1983 Bonnie Tyler's "I Need a Hero"
played in the background as Bo drove his motorcycle
kidnapping Fancy Face at her wedding.
She hopped on his motorcycle
saving her from making the worst mistake of her life.

In 1983 my abuela, the retired executive assistant,
practiced her English and politicked on my behalf to Sister
Catherine
She's smart, knows how to add and subtract, knows her alphabet.

But does she speak English?

No.

In 1983 Maria Virginia García Lozada saved Sister Catherine
from making the worst mistake of her holy career and
I started kindergarten at St. Anthony's,
entered Mrs. Farrell's pre-Pinterest days classroom
and sat in the back next to Rebecca and Vanessa
who unbeknownst to them instantly became my interpreters

and best friends.

In the summer of 1984 Steve Johnson aka Patch met Kayla
and I no longer cared about Bo and Hope.

Every day at 1pm, I watched the sand fall through the
hourglass.
For one hour, Salem was my escape from this new home
where firetrucks and police sirens interrupted my sleep
versus coquís.

Salem, where all things could happen at a pub or hospital.
Comas, amnesia, women forgetting they gave birth,
Stefano DiMera never ran out of money, Roman and Marlena
never died,
and the Bradys were the tragic family
Shakespeare could only dream about.
Salem is where I learned English.

In the fall of 1984
I greeted a shocked Sister Catherine with a "good morning"
strutted into Mrs. Dio's first grade class
and sat in the front row.

Possessive Pronouns Living Their Best Life

You are my first edition
no one else gets to write notes in your margins
hold you close, inhale your scent,
palm your pages,
know how you begin & end.

Shonda Buchanan

Poem of Hope I

(in the time of COVID-19)

Who else feels like
you are hurtling
through space
in your own spaceship,
ripping an unlooped halo
through muffled black night?

Pausing only to stop
at the grocery store,
to thank angel workers
who can't stay home,
then drive, drive, drive
the emptied streets
talking to God.

Who else
is writing a poem
of hope over despair?

Teaching your babies at home
then giggling
with friends and strangers
through moist masks.

Who else is ordering food online
for your elders
kissing them through screen doors,
stardust and bible pages...

You, my love, my friend
my human.

You will get through this.
We will get through this.
Work, sleep, dance, sing.

But don't forget to dream...
Get back in your spaceship.
set a course for Jupiter.
Keep your eyes
on the naked stars...

Poem of Hope II

(for my grandson in the time of Covid)

Every heart in the world
is my heart beating
in his hands.

Liquid stars pour from my eyes
in our video calls
and like a spider
I weave African and Indian
songs into his Taurus hair
hoping the sound of my voice
keeps time with the metronome
of his breathing.

I kiss the air as if it understands
a grandmother's love.

I kiss his eyes through
a glittery screen
and pray this will
all be over soon.

This is not the world he should inherit.
It's so hard not to hop
on an airplane,
any C-19 infested airplane
just to watch him take his
first steps. But I stay home.
Wouldn't you?

I click my heels.
Furiously shake
the snowglobes of the world
choosing a country,
any country
I want to one day visit
with him.
My grandson
I write. I dream. I surrender.
I practice silence like an art
for him
this delicate wolfbear boy
who has my heart
has me, a warrior poet,
eating
out of the palm of his hand.

Instructions on How to Make a Gun

(When Nina Simone wrote "Mississippi Goddam" in response to the Birmingham Four bombing.)

Listen to radio. Hear the news.
Try to dodge announcer's words
that shoot out of mesh and metal
entering my veins like Georgia
snake venom. Can't.
Shake head. Disbelieve cotton
muffled words echoing. Can't. Go
to basement. Find a hammer.
Get a screw driver. A saw. Tape them
together with some nails and glue. Weapon
falls apart. Nina stumbles.

God, why?
I can't take it. I gotta make a weapon.
Gotta kill some white people. Gotta

do something. Sit down at piano.
Remember little girl hands. Eight in all.
Remember Tyron, North Carolina
segregation lines that slit the backs
of your grandfathers like a blade they couldn't see.
Remember Julliard, and Curtis Institute.
Never good enough for them. Write
it with your spit. Let salt and bone
fall upon keys. Point piano and voice at them.
Grease keys in sweat and rain
of blackest nights coming.

Sing long into Harlem night
until voice is hoarse, until whiskey
has evaporated from blood.

Survival of all Things

I want to be light
I want to pass through the hands of priestesses
I want to rise in the morning with no electronics to crank
I want to be light in my heart
I want to be light in my love. Light.
I want my heart to pump sunlight blood
I want to be pure newborn breath
I want to be wet shafts of light stolen by a thirsty bear
I want to be fireflies light in a field.
Light of a hundred shields
         protecting women
Light of a thousand river rocks at dawn
Light between the lips of lovers before the first kiss
Light. light. Light.

What's my name?

(For Nina's Grandmother and Patsey in 12 Years a Slave)

No mirror
No lotion
No comb

Pulling your woman self together at the seams
was different then

No sanitary napkins
No wedding ring
No stove

Every sunset you lay down not knowing

No soap
No vaseline
No deodorant

When cold hands or a soft tap on door
would remind you

No light switch
No toothpaste
No towel

Of the coin someone bit on your behalf

No solace
No bathroom door

No hot comb

Of the weighed wet life you and your daughters and their
daughters would lead

No shampoo
No underwear
No bra

Of the salted heart in your chest when another girl was born

No bowl
No spoon
No home
The sky your only ball gown, butterflies your earrings, clouds
your abacus

No tears
No water

Only a tearing sound. We will live.

What's my name?

Someone, please tell me my name.

Teresa Mei Chuc (Chúc Mỹ Tuệ)

Quan Âm on a Dragon

Mother shows me a lacquered painting on a plaque
of Quan Âm, bodhisattva of compassion, riding a dragon.

It is misty around the bodhisattva and the dragon.
The picture looks so real, almost like a photo.

A sacred vase in one hand and a willow branch
in the other to bless devotees with the divine nectar of life.

Mother says that she and other boat refugees saw Quan Âm as we were
fleeing Vietnam after the war in a freight boat with 2,450 refugees.

When she looked up towards Heaven, in the clouds, she saw
the bodhisattva in her white, flowing robe riding a dragon.

Mother says that the goddess was there to guide and save us
from the strong waves of the South China Sea. I should know

better than to believe her though she swears it's true.
I ask again and she nods, says really, I saw Quan Âm in the clouds

as we were escaping. I should know better than to believe her.
But, a part of me wants to believe in a bodhisattva, in compassion

riding on a mythical creature, to believe that somehow something
more than just our mere human selves wanted us to live.

Cockroaches

A proposal by someone to my mom
after the Vietnam War: *Why don't
you sell your baby, you don't have
anything to eat?*

A response by my four-year-old brother:
*No, don't sell my sister! There are lots
of cockroaches for us to eat!*

When I returned to the country
eighteen years later, I saw them —
large, brown shiny tanks on the wall,

evidence of my brother's love for me.

Agent Blue

To kill correctly
takes calculation.

Down to a science.
Arsenic
cacodylic acid.

Know water and rice
on a cellular level.

Make sure
no surviving
seed can be
collected
and planted.

Because even
a small seed
assures
survival.

Because
mortars,
grenades
and bombs
can not destroy
a grain.

Because our
heart is made

of seeds.

Know what it
takes to kill
the seeds.

Know what it
takes to deprive
the plant of water,
to dehydrate it.

To be surrounded
by love but unable
to absorb it.

I Took Nothing

and broke it in half.
As if mocking me,
there was an
even greater
nothing and I
felt myself falling.

I took my falling
and broke it
in half. It did
not stop the falling.
I plunge deeper.

I took this depth
and gathered it,
the darkness
with all of its
stars, and
put it in the wings
of a bat.
I watched it
retreat into
the deepest
of caves
where it screams
and listens to
its voice
returning
from stone walls.

Photosynthesis

How can I convince you
that you do have chlorophyll,
that you can take the sun's
energy and turn it into sugar?
Produce something sweet inside of you.
Take the waste people breathe out
and make it into something that
will keep you alive, that will keep
those around you alive, create oxygen.

Why do you say that this metaphor
doesn't work, that you don't have
the powers of a plant, that nature
didn't intend you that way?

Look, how you twist and turn
towards the light.

Viva Padilla

xolo. a mi amante que ya no puede vivir debajo del capitalismo y la farsa de la democracia de los estados unidos.

si regresas a tu pueblo
diles que ahí vengo

si regresas a tu casa
diles que al pájaro no abandonas

si regresas a tu cama
diles que yo caliento tus escalofríos

cuando llego y si te encuentro
trabajando

con el peso de esos huesos
diles que tienes un recuerdo de un suspiro profundo

y deja tu labor en la esquina

la extranjera

sola por las calles camino
la extranjera soy

me dicen que merezco esto
que en todos lados menos en misa estoy

me dieron vida
en Sur Centro Los Ángeles
en América

donde las esquinas me ofrecen lana
donde sí quiero
mujer soy 40 veces al día

donde en la casa no hoy casa
donde la familia vendió todo menos la madera del techo que
tiene artritis ya

dicen que por ahí en Tecomán
cuerpos muertos no hablan por días

pero acá
cuerpos vivos no hablan por años

de uno se infectó el otro,
por esta glotona guerra de drogas

no me encuentro aquí ni allá
ni en la luna

tiene que ver un lugar para mí
me han dicho
tiene que ver un lugar para mi alma
he oído

the stranger —translated by Viva Padilla

alone
through the streets I walk
I am the stranger
they say I deserve this
that I'm everywhere but in church

they gave me life in South Central Los Angeles in America
where the corners offer me cash
where if I want woman I can be 40 times a day
where at home there is no home
where the family sold everything minus the wood of the roof
with arthritis now

they say that in Tecoman
dead bodies don't speak for days
but here live bodies don't speak for years

      from one the other got infected
      through the glutton war on drugs

I don't find myself here or there
nor with the moon
there has to be a place for me, or so I've been told
there has to be a place for my soul, or so I've heard

the destroyer woman

There is a woman I know in the ghetto
who wants to destroy shit
Every day she thinks of ways to
burn down every corner of that
fucking miserable place

This woman collects cans and bottles
and she's soon to be married to
a convenient man with a
convenience store with a gas station

This marriage of convenience
will not ever result in any babymaking
of any kind
(or the encountering of any genitals)

The woman wants to see what the
oppressor has constructed, the American ghetto,
as nothing but ash

This woman plans to be driven around in a coffin
with a bottle of mezcal
drunk off her ass

sueño americano, ni que nada

Cargaste tus huesos
    cómo maletas de hierro
    sobre arena y sangre
la obscuridad te escondió y al calor
          un gran ojo mecánico
            te encontró
            te pellizco
         como si fueras sancudo

y en una hora cruzó
    todo el terreno
    que en una semana
ya casi te reclamó

         ¿Papá?
           ¿De qué soñabas?
           si eras hombre-bolsa-de-rocas
        no montaña
acá las montañas
    las matan
    no conviven con los cosmos
se convierten en carreteras o tierra
    Ah...si...regresaste   Y esta vez te hicieron tierra
te sacaron lo que te regalo el grito del sol
    y te dejaron
    Seco
    Polvo
    Tirado
    Tumba
pero más americano que nunca
        Me iré a Coquimatlán
         a tu rancho
         a regresar ese maldito sueño
       y ahí yo olvidarlo

american dream, whatever –
translated by Linda Ravenswood

You carried your bones
like iron suitcases.
Over sand and blood
the darkness hid you
and the heat.
A great mechanical eye
found you
pinched you
as if you were a mosquito.
In one hour
it'd spanned a terrain
that took you a week to cross
and almost claimed you.
Dad?
What were you dreaming of?
That you were a man-bag-of-rocks
or a mountain!?
Here mountains
do not coexist
with the cosmos
they're turn them into roads
or landscapes.
Ah ... yes ... you came back
And this time they made you land
They took that essence out
And left you the cry of the sun
And they left you
Brittleness

Dust
The discarded tomb
but more American
than ever.
Never.
I'm going to Coquimatlán
to your ranch
to return that damn dream
and forget it

utilizing google maps to triangulate the course of my desmadre over the years

First start at some hospital run by nuns in East Los

Move me over to South Central
To a house built in 1910 with an 80-year-old avocado tree
Overrun by weeds
The house never changed its bones after the Northridge earthquake /
but it's bracing itself for the Big One

The airplanes over Century Blvd. always sounded closer in the rain
The freight train to Wilmington at night disrupted my sleep
My grandpa went straight to sleep as soon as he stepped on the tracks /
that train in Colima, Mexico was known to never miss a thing

An AK-47 once killed a 8-year-old boy around 1am outside a bar
down the street from my house,
Since then i imagine angry bullets a spatial anomaly in the spacetime
continuum / there is no one ever there actually holding a gun

Dad's last song request was time to say goodbye by Andrea Bocelli
and Sarah Brightman, he said that when he fell asleep he wasn't there
anymore / he woke himself by calling my name. I was there by his side
telling him what time it was / he could feel no more pain / i swear i
could feel nothing either but it wasn't my time yet

I smoked weed on a rooftop of a converted garage in Lynwood / shaved
my head soon thereafter / the city blamed it on the comings and goings
of freight trucks / stolen panties under the seats of truck drivers / and

little cesar's being the worst pizza because you can't
eat it the next day

In torrance, i threw a halloween party in a barn in my backyard,
no one could hear it from the street / no one lived on those streets
anyway i suspected

There's no way to know now / one night many nights
truck bed / trying to find stars
wandered to who knows where there's no way to now
Never found gold / with meth heads meeting at donut shops at
dawn / 80-year-old men stuck in front of TVs at 2 o clock in the
morning / and him showing me the mustang he couldn't put back
together again / his mom begging me to marry him as she sprays
Raid all over his carpet / wandered back out of south central who
knows how

coyotes are now surrounding the car i'm in with a man whose afraid
to get high / atop a hill on the eastside / i'm always crying / He never
cries/ i walk up the hill / shake hands with the creatures and ask
them to quiet down / they roll their eyes / later in silence they agree
that the universe needs a balance

30 days after quarantine i leave my house/ i rolled a blunt with a tree
full of mockingbirds / and a Camaro full of Swans on the street /
me and Eva look at calla lilies etched onto a fence / the sky is so big
above us / i dream of a house / lawn chairs and hammocks / to make
it real

i drive back home / park atop a hill on the eastside / can't see outside
my studio with its one window / a cricket is loud somewhere in the
room / can't make pacts with creatures that won't stay still so i sleep

Chelsea Rector

Untitled

List the number of dead
Of the heart, of the heart
Cut throat

Engird in numbers,
As I say it is, like round

A little nest, a psychic sex
Expression alone

Is dangerous, the door
Is a father who said things
Is a mother who said things
Is a metaphor for unabated joy

The heart, the heart
Honestly

At the end of the day
Everything that begins as comedy
Ends as comedy

Psalm

My prayer is that you punch me
In the back of the head on my brainstem
And I go down immediately,
like a sack
Of wet chicken

finally I won't know what's comin'
You will be charged with manslaughter
(since I didn't die in my bed)

You will go to prison
For the rest of your life
The soap on your skin,
astringent

Finally I kill you, the punchline
a manic laugh the last thing
that echoes, unredeemed

Graveness, White Bougainvillea

Chemically sealed there are
Birds that die around glass,

Crow in high water,
Finch in mud

Getting quiet

Journey Into Another Realm

To make love of all your grievous errors
You've only to get whole now
Ahold of what you long for, for, for

For not painful thought-waves
As if you've never heard of mind-control beams!
Pathways of wanting got so deep —

All you can hear yourself say is breathe, breathe, breathe
This is the voice of whole, to make love of
Time and time's impossible swing

An eyebrow plucked in caring
So love is not an abstraction
Surrendered habits, into gesture, into air

And in a contour there will be desperation,
What is called, "the heart's longing"

Ars Poetica

the poem was supposed to be
the poem was supposed to be
the poem was supposed to be
the poem was supposed to be

~~the poem was~~
~~the poem was~~
~~the poem was~~
~~the poem was~~

~~this is crazy~~
~~this is crazy~~
~~this is crazy~~
~~this is crazy~~

~~Thankfully I have a headache~~
~~So as I say this I'll be gentler~~
~~To be gentle with you~~
~~Gentle, gentle, genital~~

Man, I really see you
You're baby and you want power
We are ashes of long dead stars
You want to understand a universe
That unifies the very large
And very small:

an insect is far more complicated than a star

~~The difficulty of getting~~
~~her message~~
~~Invisible~~

I want to be loved in a highly specific manner
I want to possess and consume all the things i love
I behave dangerously self destructively, out of boredom
bored because I am tired
tired because I am detached
detached because I get too attached
too attached because I feel too much
I am tired of saying I feel too much

If there isn't an eye-of-the-storm then it is not a poem.
If there is no poem in the eye of the storm then storm is not -

Wild animal
War animal

Poetry come
from the same place as prayer
Before anything is a poem
it is just high entropy
The poet
listens to everything
Of course I watched the car
You can trust me

Any gravity helps a poem
Because when the poem lands -
The poem
is a form of looking up close
behind the camera

Cross sectioning of world

There is a deep state
Scientists studying war
Accept violence, sun storm

Mental Distress (Mother's Darling), 1871

*The carbon print of a polychrome drawing from a
photograph: Darwin wanted a picture of a crying baby to
illustrate his theory on the natural facial expressions of
mental distress. The original was too small and indistinct
to reproduce in Darwin's book, so the photo was drawn
by hand and then photographed using a solar enlarger,
an early photographic enlarger that used sunlight.*

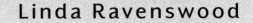

Linda Ravenswood

Bus lady

I knew a lady
out in North Hollywood
used to live
behind the Metro Station
in a car her brother left.
It had Minnesota plates
the whole thing was a rundown.
After she lost it
she ran a scam
at Greyhound
on account of getting rolled
too many times sleeping rough.
Every night
from wherever she was
she'd take a city bus
to a Greyhound Station
& fall asleep in a chair.
She'd have her suitcase at her feet
& one of those voucher sleeves
in her fist.
Anyone walking by would think
she was on her way somewhere
with her neat hat
& lime green cardigan.
But there was nothing
in the voucher jacket,
just an empty flier.
In the morning she'd
shuffle to the ladies room
freshen up & be on her way.

By the time
she was back around
to that station
it'd been a couple of weeks.
She said people thought
she was traveling
the southland.
If someone wondered
where she was going
Vegas or Reno was usually the guess.
Right on the spot
she'd make up a story
about grandbabies
keeping her on the move.
She imagined people thought
she was well loved,
waiting for her bus to be called.

After a good sleep
in her swivel chair
she'd shamble around
go to Penney's
have coffee in the flute
at Farmer's Market
or ride the RTD.
In the back of the bar
that summer I met her in Venice
she said there were two things
she thought about
nearing 80.

She missed
the old market

sitting out
among the stalls
with a big porcelain
cup of coffee.
She said wisdom
was hot coffee.
She said she missed
being young enough
to crisscross the country
on the bus.
She opened her pocketbook
& unwrapped a cloth
handkerchief
that covered her whole
face in flowers
when she wiped her chin.
She was Los Angeles.

Poetry is a Shapeshifter

Poetry must be a singer.
To remain relevant, Poetry must be liquid.
Must penetrate many crevices of society
must present itself in many genres, and on many platforms
must raise its head from traditional ideas, modes and venues
must cling within the souls of the artists
but race to merge with the souls of the People;
Poetry must be unafraid,
bold, Poetry must sing

Poetry must embrace multidimensionality and multi-genre-ality
must be liberal, but fierce in its disciplines
must have a champion
must speak history
must be indiscreet
must be tactless, falling down stairs like a toddler —
slipping into ravines like a dancer on high alert —
forgetting the words but remembering the way.
Poetry must be improvised from years of preparation
must be improvised from the genetic memory,
Poetry must be.
Poetry must be.

Poetry must be politic
must have muscles
must bend low to serve the People,
not just aggrandize the poet
must have a big heart
and a great sense of humor
must travel light, but bring

invisible cables of lineage,
culture, resistance, and resilience.
The poet must dance with everyone,
her duty not to factions —
Zhe should sing with the Tongva,
the Gabrielino, the Mexican, the Spanish,
The German, The Irish, The Jewish, The Hmong,
The Japanese, The Ethiopian, The Laotian
from the depths of poverty
and from the hope of a just wealth
from the streets and from the salon.

The poet's hair
if she has hair —
her arms
if she possess them —
her eyes
if they be —
must belong to her
though they be recycled
from a hundred other sources.
From these vessels
and others
she will nourish the People

The poet should know the land.
understand Chavez Ravine and Dodger Stadium
and speak with mercy and generosity
towards both civic realities
Zhe must stretch imaginations,
causes, firmaments, destinies —
search out justice
amendments

reparations
forgivenesses
concords
and ultimate humynhood
She must not be pigeonholed by politics
but use politics to resound fervent truths
to share place and re + member hope

The poet should live here
in this gloriastic chasm
between student and teacher
shaman and servant, magician and fool.
She must dance here
and bow to all dissemblers and non believers

(We) must travel light but like lightning;
must bring the force of light with us,
have stamina, strength, hope, vigilance, sight —
(We) must speak from the memory of place,
through personal trauma, for untapped dreams
only dared in crossed fingers and quick breaths.

It is essential the poet be a mixed person
maybe even dropped on her head once or twice
maybe her father left
or stayed
or couldn't speak
and another language had to be met
maybe her mother was a circus rider
or she went to the pictures instead of Calculus
maybe her teeth were knocked in
or she lay in Orthopaedic Hospital all of 3rd grade
maybe she saw a man beaten on a corner

out of the corner of her eye
and she never dis+remembered —

it is essential that the poet live in this liminal place,
towards a wholeness of humanity

If the poet can be a person of multiple heritages
with allegiances to all —
If the poet can be college-educated
someone who experiences prison
a world traveler
a seamstress
a high school dropout
live out of their car
or on the beach

If zhe knows Dante's Trail, Biddy Mason, The Mattachine
Steps, Florence & Normandie, the Magic Castle, Nickerson
Gardens, ONE Gallery, the paleteros of Boyle Heights, Hop
Louie's, Smitty's Liquor, the Saugus Cafe, Belmont Heights,
Llano del Rio, Geoffrey's in Malibu, Mtrice Richardson,
Angels Flight, the Pacific Red Car, The La Brea Tar Pits, The
Farmers Market before The Grove, Ray Bolger's dance at Good
Shepherd Church, The Pink Lady of the Canyon, what the
Third Street Promenade looked like before 1995, where Tony
Curtis filmed in Los Feliz, the California Incline, Leimert Park
& The World Stage, when you could swim in Santa Monica,
the South Central Farm

If the poet can know
If he can remember
If the poet can sing
If they can be an old man and a young woman

If they can be an old woman and a young man
because —
Poetry must be.
Poetry must be.

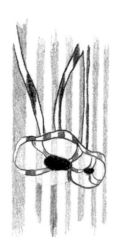

Gen X Suite

We are Gen X
we never get old I mean
we get old but we never crack
like the rest
we Gen X
we look younger than millennials
sorry millennials
why don't you
plug in your car
and emo up
it'll be just a sec til
both your parents / still married
come help

we're Gen X
we loved those rockers on MTV
so much that we got with them
followed them
tried to be like them
married them
took them from their sad Reseda houses
and injected them with new energy
vitality
hope

we're Gen X
we breed false hope

we are Gen X
we have no money

but our dicks still work

We Gen X
they could smell it
on us
all the earlier rockers
smelled it
wanted to get with us
quote - *the minute I saw you*
I knew I wanted to have a baby with you - end quote
we are Gen X
you see your unborn children in our eyes

we're Gen X
we common law married
old rockers
and trust funders and bartenders
married your big hair
and your big dreams
your big stories of Oregon
and the bend in the Snake River —
we married you white boy
married you Ratt, Poison, Cinderella,
married you TJ Hooker
married you 2 Live Crew

you loved us
but you could never
be us
like the elders loved the Beats
but were destined for the GM factory floor —
man did you want us
saw Kurt Cobain magic on us

knew wet Seattle and Aberdeen
knew everything we know
but you not Gen X -
we Gen X see -

you could never be us
could never know
that particular turn-of-the-century loneliness
that latchkey Kid show
that eye drop tear drop sugar drop

we were raised by Skittles

We're Gen X
and now we are alone
nodding to each other at the farmers market
the grove, the americana,
(what is Los Angeles)
L.A. Cum Disneyland
now all LA
is Disney covered
we look
we nod
we make our hand thump
we do joint break
we drop low
we look 30 ... ish
but really
we so much older.

epilogue

goodbye Tom Petty –
we hardly knew you –
goodbye to all your heart break too
goodbye Tom Petty
and all the guys who look like you
goodbye to you –
and all the boys
who look like you

this message has no body

& if they took away your iPhone your helper your slave /
that which enslaves others / that you use with so much
oblivious gratitude which means America / would you still
be you / & if they took away your rented house in a rented
part of town because your parents did not believe in you
enough for a down payment on your piece of the dream /
would you still be you / & if they took away your car / the one
that was better than the other so you had to sleep in the car
that was the lesser of two evils / would you still be you /
& if they took away your high-heeled shoes & your Fendi
bag & your deodorant / & you huffed down streets & hobbled
hello to strangers faces / meal tickets and brine / wondering
where running water lives / would you still be you /
& if they took away your children / your friends / anyone
who knew your name / given & carried all these years
/ a deck of cards at a carnival shell game between who you are
& how you ache // seamstress of prostitutes & taxi drivers /
crock pot whistleblower / former endless cocksucker / mid-life
failure / nameless in the city of names // would you still be
you / & if they took away your sight so all you had was the breeze
/ when the breeze / if the breeze / & the sound of pigeon on pavement
/ would you still be you / & if they took away the skin of you /
your wax paper show / your outer coating / your reviled worst name /
would you still be you /

If I was smart as an onion skin

If I was smart as an onion skin
they wouldn't have gotten to me —
they might've smelled me
but they wouldn't have gotten
inside. I'd have kept my coat on
and they wouldn't't've dared break it open —
my loud onion skin coat
would've rattled down their hands
and instead of trying to pull it off
they'd've been keeping it quiet
and straight. If I was an onion smart girl
I wouldn't't've shown my green secret
and my ruffle fringe. I'd have
smiled with my whole face around
and they never would've seen the end of it.

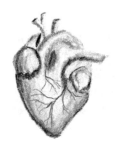

BIOS

Kohenet **Rachel Kann** is a devotional poet and ceremonialist.
She was the 2020 New England Jewish Poetry Festival's
Featured Poet and a 2020 Cosmic Sister "Women of The
Psychedelic Renaissance" awardee for her poetry presentation
at the 2020 Spirit Plant Medicine Conference.

She is a WORD: Bruce Geller Memorial Prize recipient for
How to Bless the New Moon, from Ben Yehuda Press. Previous
books include *You Sparkle Inside*, (an illustrated kids' book,)
A Prayer on Behalf of the Broken Heart, (a collection of Jewish
poetry) and the mixed genre *10 For Everything*. Her poetry and
fiction appear in journals including *Hevria, Eclipse, Permafrost,
Coe Review, Sou'wester, GW Review, Quiddity*, and *Lalitamba*.
Find her work in anthologies *A Poet's Haggadah, Word Warriors*
from Seal Press, *His Rib* from Penmanship Press, and *Knocking
at the Door* from Birch Bench Press.

Her spoken word film, *The Quickening*, has received accolades
from film festivals in Florence, Tel Aviv, Los Angeles and New
York.

She's performed her poetry in venues such as Disney Concert
Hall, Royce Hall, The Broad Stage, The San Francisco Palace of
Fine Arts and TEDxUCLA.

Poet Laureate Editor-in-Chief Emerita of Altadena, California (2018 to 2020), **Teresa Mei Chuc (Chúc Mỹ Tuệ)** is the author of three full-length collections of poetry, *Red Thread* (Fithian Press, 2012), *Keeper of the Winds* (FootHills Publishing, 2014) and *Invisible Light* (Many Voices Press, 2018). She was born in Saigon, Vietnam and immigrated to the U.S. under political asylum with her mother and brother shortly after the Vietnam War while her father remained in a Vietcong "reeducation" prison camp for nine years. Since the age of two, Teresa grew up in the Tongva village of Hahamongna (Pasadena, California) where she still lives and loves. Teresa is a graduate of the Masters in Fine Arts in Creative Writing program (Poetry) at Goddard College in Plainfield, Vermont and teaches literature and writing at a public high school in Los Angeles.

Chelsea Rector is a poet living and working in Los Angeles, CA. Her work has appeared in the Los Angeles Press, and in publication with Rebel Hands Press (Cry List, 2019). Her manifesto On Being Mean will be published by RHP in Spring, 2021. For poems visit crimpingiron.tumblr.com. She is the co-founder of P/SICHO ST THEATER COMPANY (est. 2018), an experimental text and performance project with artist Jeremy Kennedy. The company released episodes 1-3 of the radio play, 'Beglitched,' in 2020.

Born in Beirut, Lebanon, **Arminé Iknadossian**'s family sought political asylum in California when she was four years old to escape the civil war. She earned her English degree with an emphasis in creative writing from UCLA and later completed her MFA in poetry at Antioch University. Iknadossian is the author of the chapbook United States of Love & Other Poems (2015) and the full-length collection All That Wasted Fruit (Main Street Rag). Her poetry has recently been included in *Whale Road Review, Southern Florida Poetry Journal, KYSO Flash/MacQueen's Quarterly, The American Journal of Poetry*. She has received fellowships from Idyllwild Arts, The Los Angeles Writing Project and Otis College of Art and Design. She facilitates writing workshops for Surprise the Line and lives in Long Beach, California.

Luivette Resto, a mother, teacher, poet, and Wonder Woman fanatic, was born in Aguas Buenas, Puerto Rico but proudly raised in The Bronx. Her two books of poetry Unfinished Portrait and Ascension have been published by Tía Chucha Press. Some of her latest work can be found in the anthology titled What Saves Us: Poems of Empathy and Outrage in the Age of Trump edited by Martín Espada and on the University of Arizona's Poetry Center website. She lives in the San Gabriel Valley with her three children aka her revolutionaries.

Author of five books, including Black Indian, **Shonda Buchanan** is a daughter of Mixed Bloods, tri-racial and tri-ethnic African American, American Indian and European-descendant families who migrated from North Carolina and Virginia in the mid-1700 to 1800s to Michigan. Black Indian, her memoir, which won the Indie New Generation Book Award for Memoir was chosen by PBS NewsHour, as top 20 books about institutional racism. Her collection of poetry, Who's Afraid of Black Indians? was nominated for the Black Caucus of the American Library Association and the Library of Virginia Book Awards. An award-winning poet and educator, Shonda is a Sundance Writing Arts Fellow, a California Community Foundation Fellow, a PEN Emerging Voices Fellow, Literary Editor of Harriet Tubman Press and Vice President of the Board for Beyond Baroque Literary Arts Center.

In addition to her work as a literary activist, a teaching artist and a mentor for young writers, she's taught at Hampton University, William & Mary College, California State University, Northridge and Mt. San Antonio College. Finishing a collection of poetry about Nina Simone, Shonda received an MFA at Antioch University and teaches at her alma mater, Loyola Marymount University. She lives and writes in Los Angeles. Follow her @shondabuchanan and www.ShondaBuchanan.com

Allison Adelle Hedge Coke she left school to work in the fields as a child, she later attended North Carolina State University, Estelle Harmon's Actor's Workshop, Jack Kerouac School of Disembodied Poetics Summer Writing Program, and earned an AFAW in creative writing from the Institute for American Indian Arts and an MFA from Vermont College. She is the author of the poetry chapbook *Year of the Rat* (1996); the full-length poetry collections *Dog Road Woman* (1997), *Off-Season City Pipe* (2005), *Blood Run* (2006 UK, 2007 US), *Streaming* (2014), an illustrated (by Dustin Illetewahke Mater) special edition *Burn* (2017); and the memoir *Rock, Ghost, Willow, Deer* (2004, 2014). Streaming comes with a full album recorded in the Rd Klā project period with Kelvyn Bell and Laura Ortman. One inclusion was selected by Motion Poems and Pixel Farms to be made into an animated film and several of the poems in *Streaming* also influenced the film she is currently in-production directing, *Red Dust*.

Viva Padilla is a poet and founding editor of *Dryland*, an independent print literary journal founded in South Central Los Angeles in 2015. She is a first-generation Chicana, daughter of Mexican immigrants who crossed the border. She has been in the trenches at the *LA Times*, Red Hen Press, and Punk Hostage Press. Her poetry has been featured in *Coiled Serpent: Poets Arising from LA's Cultural Quakes & Shifts* (Tia Chucha Press), *Acentos Review*, Brooklyn & Boyle and others. Last October, she was featured at Casa De Las Americas in Havana, Cuba. She is currently working on a bilingual poetry manuscript.

In 2021, **Lynne Thompson** was appointed Poet Laureate for the City of Los Angeles. Thompson is the author of *Start With a Small Guitar, Beg No Pardon*, winner of the Perugia Book Award and the Great Lakes Colleges New Writers Award, and Fretwork, selected by Jane Hirshfield for the Marsh Hawk Poetry Prize. Her recent work appears or is forthcoming in *Ploughshares, New England Review, Pleiades, december, and Black Warrior Review*. Thompson serves on the Boards of Cave Canem and the Los Angeles Review of Books.

Linda Ravenswood (BFA, MA, PhD abd) is a poet and
performance artist. Founder and EIC of The Los Angeles
Press, Linda was shortlisted for Poet Laureate of Los Angeles
in 2017. A Pushcart nominee for Poetry and Short Story, she
serves on The California Arts Council, is a California Writers
Project winner, and Master of Ceremonies at The Poetry
Brothel (a project of The Poetry Society of New York). A
collection of poetry, **rock waves / sloe drags** will be published
in Winter 2021 by Eyewear London. A two volume poetry
collection, **The Stan Poems, Indictments** and **The Stan
Poems, Amendments** is forthcoming from Pedestrian Press
in Summer 2021. Linda is also a curriculum designer and
educator (UCLA, Occidental College), teaching at over 60 LA
County schools each year. Like many authors in *XLA*, Linda
is of mixed Indigenous and European ancestry (NDN/First
Nation (Pokanoket, Wampanoag) & Mayflower immigrants
on her mother's side & Indigenous/*Mestizaje y hijas de corsarios
de Baja California Sur* on her father's side). She was raised in
Los Angeles by Jewish Holocaust survivors from WWII.

Find her at thelosangelespress.com
and on Instagram @TheLosAngelesPress

Look for the <u>X LA Poets</u> E-book. Available at
www.hinchaspress.com

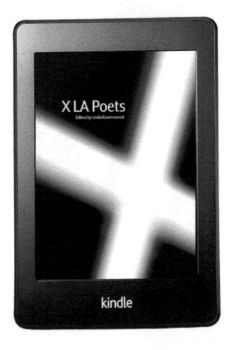

ISBN: 978-1-7324848-9-4

More titles from HINCHAS Press

Inspiring Library Stories: Tales of Kindness, Connection, and Community Impact

Edited by Oleg Kagan
ISBN: 978-1732484863

Librarians With Spines Books

www.librarianswithspines.com

Zines from HINCHAS Press

Zine Subscriptions

Get the latest zines from HINCHAS Press delivered to you every month!

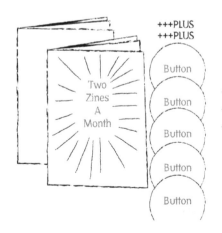

Choose your subscription plan:

- Regular Subscription
- Regular Plus Subscription
- Regular Plus Plus Subscription

Coming Soon from HINCHAS Press

- Librarians With Spines Vol. III- Lowrider Librarian Edition
- Quarenzine Project

The James Foley Scriptorium
is an extremely small library and
zine manuscript laundry room
located down a nondescript
driveway in Mar Vista, Los
Angeles. The Scriptorium is
dedicated to collecting fiction and
non-fiction that American Combat
Journalist James Foley might have
lent you, or suggested you read.

The zines donated, in exchange, to the James Foley Scriptorium will get added
to the local LAPL zine collection of the West Los Angeles Regional Library (11360
Santa Monica Blvd., 90025).

To participate scan the QR code or go to
hinchaspress.com/james-foley-scriptorium.

Look for <u>Ghazals for Foley</u> by Yago Cura

HINCHAS
Press

www.HINCHASpress.com